PR!DE
IN LONDON

ABC
PRIDE

Written by
Dr Elly Barnes MBE and Louie Stowell

Illustrations by
Amy Phelps

How to use this book

Follow the alphabet from A to Z while discovering the wonderful world of Pride.

Find questions at the back to inspire more conversations and learning.

Join the party and feel the

PRIDE!

A is for **acceptance**

When you accept yourself and other people accept you for who you are.

B is for **belonging**

When you know you are in the right place, surrounded by the things you love, and the people who make you feel good.

C is for **celebrate**

Life is full of amazing moments and wonderful people. We should all celebrate each other!

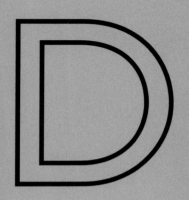

D is for **difference**

No two people are the same. Meeting new people and learning more about people everywhere is always exciting.

E is for **equity**

When we give everyone the things they need to do the things they want to in life.

F is for **flag**

There are lots of flags that people use to show who they are.

G is for **gender**

Something people guess about you based on how you dress or how your body looks. But you know best who you are.

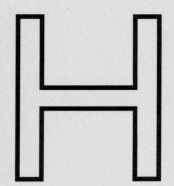is for **human rights**

All humans have the right to live how they want. Some people need help, because their rights have been taken away.

is for **icon**

Someone special — usually a famous person — who you, and lots of other people, want to be like.

J is for justice

Making sure everyone is treated fairly to give them the same chance to be successful.

K is for **kindness**

Doing nice things to help make other people's lives better, like sharing your favourite toy.

is for **love**

Love is a feeling you have for someone who is very special to you. You can love whoever you want – or no one, as not everyone falls in love.

M is for **march**

Some people march in the streets to tell others about something that is important to them or something they think is unfair.

# N is for **non-binary**
A word for a person who doesn't
see themselves as a particular gender.

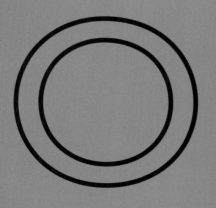 **is for out**

Being "out" means telling other people about your gender or who you love.

P is for **pride**

Being a confident LGBTQ+ person and happy with who you are.

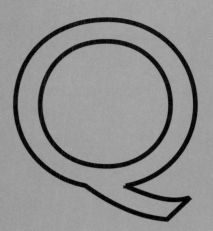

Q is for **questioning**

It's okay not to know your gender and who you love or don't love. Your feelings might change too, and that's okay.

R is for **rainbow**

The rainbow flag is a special sign for all LGBTQ+ people. The stripes mean love, healing, sunlight, nature, harmony, and spirit.

 is for **stereotypes**

When you think you know who a person is and what they feel because of the way they look. Clothes and colours are for everyone!

T is for **trans**

Someone whose gender does not match what was written on their birth certificate when they were born.

 is for **understanding**
Listening to what other people say about themselves helps you to understand them.

V is for **values**

Values are things you think are important, like honesty, kindness, taking turns, sharing, and thinking about other people's feelings.

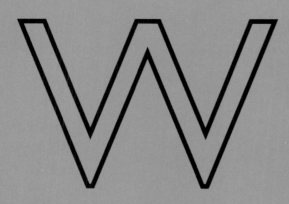

W is for **wig**

Fake hair that some people wear for fun, to show who they are, and to make them feel good.

X is for **xe** *(pronounced zee)*

We all use pronouns to talk about someone without using their name, such as she, he, or they. Some people use xe instead.

Y is for **you**

You are a wonderful person,
whoever you are. Always be you!

Z is for **zero**

The number of people
we want to be unhappy.

DISCUSSION

For parents, caregivers, and teachers to start up conversations with little ones.

Difference

How are your friends different from you?

Equity

How could you help someone
to achieve the things they want?

Icon

Who do you look up to?

Kindness

How could you help others if
they were being treated unfairly?

March

What rights would you march for?

Questioning

What questions do you have
about the LGBTQ+ community?

Rainbow

What do the colours
mean to you?

Stereotypes

Can you name something
that may be a stereotype?

Values

What's important to you?

Wig

Which clothes make
you feel good?

Xe

Practise saying some
pronouns together.

DK | Penguin Random House

Editor Vicky Armstrong
Project Art Editor Chris Gould
Production Editor Marc Staples
Production Controller Louise Minihane
Senior Acquisitions Editor Katy Flint
Managing Art Editor Vicky Short
Publishing Director Mark Searle

First published in Great Britain in 2022
by Dorling Kindersley Limited
One Embassy Gardens, 8 Viaduct Gardens, London SW11 7BW
A Penguin Random House Company

Dorling Kindersley Limited
DK, a Division of Penguin Random House LLC
10 9 8 7 6 5 4 3 2
002–332043–June/22

PR!DE
IN LONDON

The authorized representative in the EEA is Dorling Kindersley Verlag GmbH.
Arnulfstr. 124, 80636 Munich, Germany

A CIP catalogue record for this book is available from the British Library.
ISBN 978-0-2415-7254-2

Printed and bound in China

Acknowledgements
Thanks to the authors, Dr Elly Barnes MBE and Louie Stowell, for their text. This title was created with support from the DK Diversity, Equity, and Inclusion team. Thanks to the Product and Content Working Group for their input and guidance. DK would also like to thank Fox Fisher and Leon Wenham for consulting on this title, and Rosie Peet for editorial assistance.

For the curious

www.dk.com